Editors
Lorin Klistoff, M.A.
Kathleen "Casey" Petersen

Managing Editor
Karen Goldfluss, M.S. Ed.

Illustrator
Renée Christine Yates

Cover Artist
Brenda DiAntonis

Art Manager
Kevin Barnes

Art Director
CJae Froshay

Imaging
Alfred Lau
Rosa C. See

Publisher
Mary D. Smith, M.S. Ed.

Math in Measurement
Grades 1-2

· Hands-on activities · Easy-to-use manipulatives · Lessons & objectives included

Author

Bev Dunbar

(Revised and rewritten by Teacher Created Resources, Inc.)

This edition published by *Teacher Created Resources, Inc.*
6421 Industry Way
Westminster, CA 92683
www.teachercreated.com

ISBN-1-4206-3532-8

©2005 Teacher Created Resources, Inc.

Made in U.S.A.

Teacher Created Resources

Table of Contents

Introduction

Measurement is an important aspect of any mathematics program. It is a practical way to apply number skills to solve problems specific to each student's stage of development. Both the classroom and the playground can be utilized, and a wide variety of everyday objects can be used as measuring objects.

Math in Action: Measurement includes many action-packed ideas for developing skills in exploring, comparing, and using informal units in fun, practical ways. The activities can range from simple to super-challenging, to help support different ability groups.

Making your teaching life easier is a major aim of this series. The book is divided into sequenced units. The units contain activity cards and worksheets for small groups or a whole class to explore. You will also find easy-to-follow instructions, with assessment help in the form of clearly stated skills linked to a record sheet (pages 93–94).

Each activity is designed to maximize the way in which your students construct their own understanding about length, area, volume, and mass. The activities are generally open-ended and encourage each student to think and work mathematically. The emphasis is always on practical manipulation of materials and the development of individual recording skills, rather than just writing answers into a textbook.

Have fun exploring length, area, volume, and mass with your students.

How to Use This Book

❑ **Teaching Ideas**

More than 50 exciting teaching ideas have been divided into fourteen sections to assist your lesson planning for the whole class or small groups. Each activity has clear learning outcomes and easy-to-follow instructions. Activities are open-ended and encourage your students to think for themselves.

❑ **Reproducible Pages**

In this book are over 60 reproducible pages. Below are some examples of different types of pages which are included in this book.

Reusable Resources

(e.g., page 11, What Is Nearer?)
These resources support free exploration, as well as structured activities. Laminate them for reuse with small groups.

Discussion Cards

(e.g., page 77, Is It Heavier?)
Cut these out, shuffle, and use over and over again for small group games. Copy each set in a different color.

Activity Cards

(e.g., page 43, Which Covers More?)
Use these as an additional stimulus in group work. The language is simple and easy-to-follow. Encourage your students to invent their own activity cards, too.

Sample Recording Sheets

(e.g., page 35, Flying Far)
These provide reusable examples to support the development of students' own recording skills.

❑ **Skills Record Sheet**

The complete list of learning outcomes is available on pages 93–94. Use this to record individual student progress.

❑ **Sample Weekly Lesson Plan**

On page 95 you will find an example of how to organize a selection of activities for Comparing Lengths as a five-day unit for your class. A blank weekly lesson plan is included on page 96 for individual use.

Exploring Length Language

In this unit, your students will do the following:

- ❏ Construct, describe, and recognize long/short lengths
- ❏ Construct, describe, and recognize high/low lengths
- ❏ Construct, describe, and recognize thick/thin lengths
- ❏ Construct, describe, and recognize wide/narrow lengths
- ❏ Construct, describe, and recognize deep/shallow depths
- ❏ Describe and recognize near/far distances

(The skills in this section are listed on the Skills Record Sheet on page 93.)

Sausage Dog

Skills

- ❏ Construct, describe, and recognize long/short lengths
- ❏ Construct, describe, and recognize high/low lengths

Grouping

- ❏ small groups
- ❏ whole class

Materials

- ❏ photo of a dachshund *(optional)*
- ❏ crayons or colored pencils
- ❏ copy of Sausage Dog head and tail (page 7)
- ❏ glue or tape
- ❏ pencils
- ❏ scissors
- ❏ 8½" x 11" paper

Directions

- ❏ Have students list as many long creatures as they can within one minute. (e.g., snake, worm, centipede, weasel)
- ❏ Discuss dachshunds. Ask students, "What is special about this sort of dog?" (e.g., They have long bodies but very short legs. They are not very high off the ground.) Ask students, "Why are they sometimes called sausage dogs?"
- ❏ Tell students to imagine if these dogs could grow longer and longer. Tell students that they will make a long sausage dog together. Show the head and tail. Discuss how the middle part of the body is missing.
- ❏ Each person folds and cuts a sheet of paper into four pieces. These are missing parts of the sausage dog's body. Have students color and decorate the pieces.
- ❏ Have students construct a very long sausage dog as a class display using the head and tail with all the decorated body parts in between.

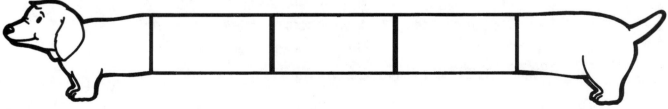

Variations

- ❏ Have students write stories about the adventures of this very long dog.
- ❏ Make more copies of the dachshund head and tail. Have students construct more than one dog and compare the lengths of the dogs.

6

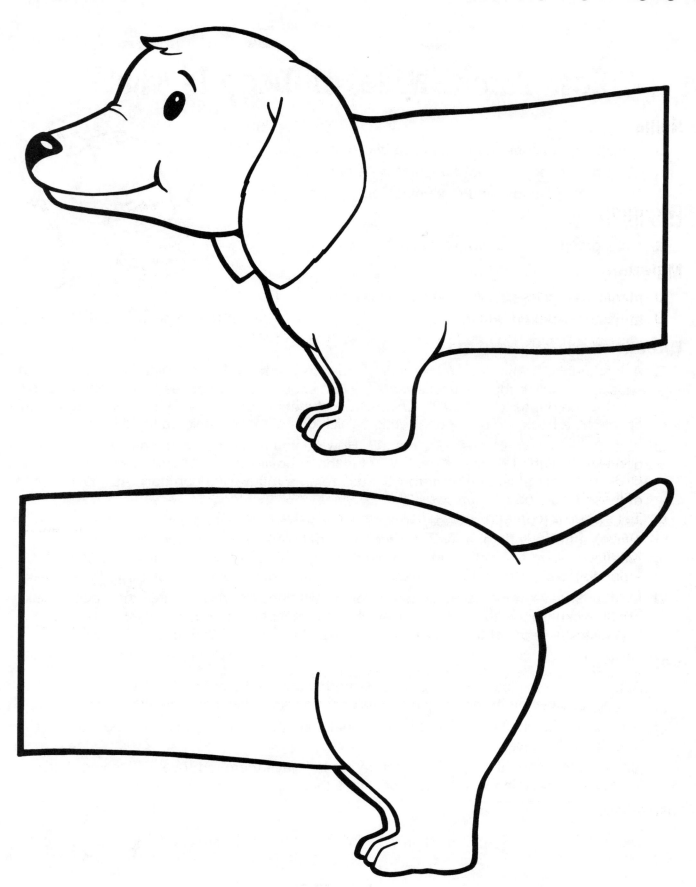

How Thick, Wide, or Deep Is That?

Skills

- ❏ Construct, describe, and recognize thick/thin lengths
- ❏ Construct, describe, and recognize wide/narrow lengths
- ❏ Construct, describe, and recognize deep/shallow depths

Grouping

- ❏ small groups
- ❏ whole class

Materials

- ❏ magazines, scissors, glue, pencils, class book
- ❏ attribute blocks (thick/thin shapes)
- ❏ play clay
- ❏ length picture cards (page 9)

Directions

- ❏ Ask students, "What does *thick* mean? How do you know if something is thick? (e.g., a sausage, a wall, a rope, a wool sweater) What about gravy or sauces? What about soup? What is the opposite of *thick*?" *(thin)* Have students name at least five thin things. (e.g., spaghetti, a book, ice on a pond) Ask, "Which one of these would be the thinnest?"
- ❏ Ask students, "What does *wide* mean? How do you know if something is wide? (e.g., a doorway, a path, a ribbon, a gap) What is the opposite of *wide*?" *(narrow)* Have students name at least five narrow things. (e.g., a roadway, a corridor) Ask, "Which one of these would be the narrowest?"
- ❏ Ask students, "What does *deep* mean? How do you know if something is deep? (e.g., a bucket, a pond, a bath, a river, an ocean) What is the opposite word of *deep*?" *(shallow)* Have students name at least five shallow things. (e.g., a dish, a stream, a puddle) Ask, "Which one of these would be the shallowest?"
- ❏ In groups, have students cut pictures from magazines or draw pictures for a class book about thickness, width, or depth. Have them investigate more fascinating facts. (e.g., The average depth of the Pacific Ocean is 4250 meters [15,215 feet/2,881 miles].)

Variations

- ❏ Ask everyone to close their eyes. Pass around a collection of attribute blocks. Have students say whether their object is thick or thin. (e.g., I've got a small, thin triangle.)
- ❏ Have students challenge a partner to model something thick or thin with the play clay. (e.g., a thick sausage dog)
- ❏ Have students shuffle the length picture cards. Have them turn over the top card and identify the matching length concept. Have them find or name something to match.

wide 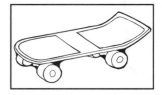   thin    shallow

#3532 Math in Action

What Is Nearer?

Skills

❑ Describe and recognize near/far distances

Grouping

❑ small groups   ❑ whole class

Materials

❑ pencils and paper
❑ near/far picture cards (page 11)
❑ a whistle *(optional)*

Directions

❑ Ask students, "What does *near* mean? Who is near to you now?" Ask students to describe some other things that are near to them. Ask, "What are some other words for *near*?" (e.g., *close, next to, beside*)

❑ Ask students, "What is the opposite of near?" *(far)* Have students describe some things that are far from them now. Ask, "What are some other words for *far*? (e.g., *at a distance from, far away, a long way away*)

❑ Ask students, "Where do you live? Is your home near to your friends? To your grandma? To our school? Who lives the closest to school? The furthest away? Who do you know who lives the furthest away from you in the whole world?"

❑ Have students draw pictures showing three things that are very near to where they are now and three things that are very far away.

Variations

❑ Have students play What Is Nearer? in small groups. Have them shuffle the picture cards. Have them select a card and answer questions from their friends. (e.g., What is the nearest object? What is closer than the sheep?)

❑ Have students play Who Is Nearest? Find a large open space. (e.g., the playground) Have students run around all over this space. Tell them to stop when they hear the signal. (e.g., a whistle) Ask them, "Who is nearest to you now? Who is the furthest away?"

What Is Furthest Away?

Skills

- ❏ Describe and recognize near/far distances
- ❏ Order three or more lengths by direct comparison

Grouping

- ❏ whole class in small groups

Materials

- ❏ What Is Furthest Away? activity cards (page 13)
- ❏ timers (e.g., stopwatch or a kitchen timer)
- ❏ balls, hoops
- ❏ markers to record lengths (e.g., yardsticks, tape measure)

Directions

- ❏ Tell students to think of songs or stories that involve the idea of far away. (e.g., "Five little ducks went out one day, over the hills and far away . . . .") Ask, "How do you know how far away that is?"
- ❏ Have students compare how far away three or more distant objects are from them now. Have them describe how they know which one is the furthest away.
- ❏ Divide students into teams. Discuss the different What Is Furthest Away? activities together. Discuss different methods for measuring and recording each team's results.
- ❏ Teams rotate around activities after a suitable time limit.
- ❏ Develop a class display of key results.

Variation

- ❏ Have students create a class book full of interesting far away facts. (e.g., Which planet is furthest away from our sun? Which country is furthest away from where we live?)

You need a 10-second timer.

How far can you run before the timer stops?

Do you go further if you walk, skip, or hop?

Who goes the furthest each time in your team?

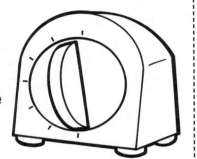

You need a ball.

How far can you throw the ball?

Do you throw further underarm or overarm?

Who can throw the furthest in your team?

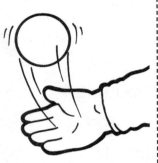

You need a hoop.

How far can you roll a hoop until it falls over?

Practice rolling it in different ways. Who can roll the furthest in your team?

How far can you jump?

Practice jumping up in different ways.

Who can jump the furthest in your team?

You need a ball for each two players.

Throw (and catch) the ball to a partner without dropping it.

How far away can you stand from each other?

Which pair can throw (and catch) the furthest in your team?

You need a ball for each two players.

Roll the ball so it goes between your partner's legs.

How far away can your partner stand?

Which pair can roll the furthest in your team?

13

Comparing Lengths

In this unit, your students will do the following:

- ❏ Compare and describe two lengths
- ❏ Identify objects with the same length
- ❏ Match baselines to make comparisons
- ❏ Order three or more lengths

(The skills in this section are listed on the Skills Record Sheet on page 93.)

Make It Longer

Skills

- ❏ Compare and describe two lengths
- ❏ Identify objects with the same length

Grouping

- ❏ up to the whole class

Materials

- ❏ Make It Longer worksheet (page 16)
- ❏ pencils

Directions

- ❏ Have students look at the eight different picture boxes. Discuss the words they would use to describe the length/height/thickness/width/depth, as appropriate.
- ❏ Have students look at the hair. Tell them to draw hair on the second child but make it longer.

   Have students look at the shoes and socks. Tell them to draw socks on the second child but make them longer.

   Have students look at the dog. Tell them to draw a longer tail on the second dog.

   Have students look at the snake. Tell them to draw a second snake that is longer.

   Have students look at the crayon. Tell them to draw a second crayon that is longer.
- ❏ Have students look at the emtpy box. Tell them to draw their own picture about something that is very long.

Variations

- ❏ Make a second copy of the worksheet. This time give instructions to make the second object shorter/shallower/lower/narrower, as appropriate.
- ❏ Make a third copy of the worksheet. This time give instructions to make the second object exactly the same length/height/thickness/width/depth, as appropriate.
- ❏ Make a fourth copy of the worksheet. This time challenge the students in pairs to give mixed instructions, using words like *taller than*, *the same length as,* or *shorter than*.

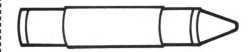

Walking Around

Skills

- ❑ Match baselines to make comparisons
- ❑ Identify objects with the same length
- ❑ Order three or more lengths

Grouping

- ❑ small groups ❑ whole class

Materials

- ❑ workbooks for recording discoveries
- ❑ Jungle Paths worksheet (page 18)
- ❑ string, yarn, scissors

Directions

- ❑ Tell students to imagine they wanted to tie a piece of string around a tree or pole in the playground. Ask them, "Which tree would need the longest string?" Demonstrate by cutting a length of string to match the distance around one tree trunk. Compare this length with strings cut to match the distance around other trees. Show students how to line up one end of each string to compare their lengths. Ask, "Was your guess close? Which tree must be the thickest? The thinnest? Are any trees the same thickness?"

- ❑ Discuss the lengths of different walkways or sidewalks at school. Ask students, "Which walkway do you think is the longest?" Have students find a way to check. Ask, "Which walkway is the widest?" Have students find a way to check.

- ❑ Discuss the distance around three or more buildings. (e.g., a shed, a portable classroom) Ask, "Which one do you think is the longest? Why?" Have students find a way to check.

- ❑ Discuss students' findings. Have them record some of their favorite discoveries.

Variations

- ❑ Discuss all the different ways students come to school. Ask, "Who travels the furthest? Who has the shortest journey?"

- ❑ Have students look at the Jungle Paths worksheet. Have them guess which animal travels the shortest distance to the waterhole. Have them guess which animal travels the longest distance. Ask, "Do you think any animals travel the same distance? How can we check?" (e.g., Cut a piece of string to match each distance and compare string lengths.) Discover, compare, and discuss the lengths of the different animal paths.

- ❑ Have students draw their own jungle path maze for a friend to use. Ask, "Can your friend guess the shortest distance to travel?"

Jungle Paths

©*Teacher Created Resources, Inc.*

Length Challenges

Skills

❑ Order three or more lengths

Grouping

❑ whole class   ❑ small groups

Materials

❑ straws; ping-pong balls; a long, flat surface

❑ paper fish (page 20); fans (books or small flat boards); a long, flat surface

❑ snails; colored dot stickers (to identify each team's snail); a long, flat surface; one-minute timer

❑ small toy cars; a long ramp (wooden board); a long, flat surface

❑ yardsticks, meter sticks, or tape measures for measuring distances

❑ Length Challenges Cards (pages 21 and 22)

❑ *(optional)* medals (gold/silver/bronze)

Directions

❑ Discuss different types of length investigations students could carry out as a class. (e.g., Is the person with the longest hair the tallest person in the class? Does the person with the longest legs have the longest stride? How can you find out?)

❑ Discuss the Olympic Games and how many events involve length. (e.g., Who can throw a javelin the longest distance? Who can jump the longest distance on the long jump?)

❑ Explain the different Length Challenge activities. Break the class into four teams. Decide on a name for each team. In turn, each team explores ways to create the longest length possible for each activity. This is the practice stage. Each team can elect its fastest member as its team's challenger.

❑ When each team has rotated through all four practice activities, the competitors from each team compete in the first Length Challenge. (e.g., How far can you blow?) The rest of the class can be the audience. (Alternately, all four activities can run at the same time with a member from each team as the competitor and other team members as supporters.)

❑ *(Optional)* Award medals to the winning teams.

Variation

❑ Have students create their own Length Challenges. Have them compete with another class. They could even have a whole school challenge!

How far can you blow?

✔ You need a straw and a ping-pong ball.

✔ What is the furthest distance you can blow the ball in one blow?

How far can it swim?

✔ You need a paper fish and a fan.

✔ Place the paper fish on a flat surface (a table or the floor). Use your fan to blow the fish across the surface.

✔ What is the furthest distance you can make a paper fish "swim" by fanning it three times?

How far can it crawl?

✔ You need a snail and a timer.

✔ What is the furthest distance the snail can crawl in one minute?

How far can it roll?

✔ Use a toy car and a ramp.

✔ What is the furthest distance you can make the car travel using the ramp?

Using Informal Length Units

In this unit, your students will do the following:

- ❏ Use informal units to estimate and measure straight lengths
- ❏ Order three or more lengths using informal units
- ❏ Use informal units to estimate and measure curves
- ❏ Use informal units to estimate and measure perimeters

(The skills in this section are listed on the Skills Record Sheet on page 93.)

Measure Monsters

Skills
❏ Use informal units to estimate and measure straight lengths

Grouping
❏ up to the whole class   ❏ pairs

Materials
❏ cardboard, scissors, colored paper, glue
❏ sample Measure Monster (equal length to the teacher's height)
❏ Measure Monsters cards (page 25), pencils

Directions
❏ Make a sample Measure Monster. Cut a cardboard strip to match your height, then use colored paper to decorate it to look like a monster.

❏ Have students name three tall students and estimate which one is the tallest. Ask, "What makes you think this?" Have them check their estimate.

❏ Tell students to imagine they could use the tallest student as a length measure. Have them estimate how many body lengths they need to measure the length of the room. Ask, "How can you check your estimate?" (e.g., Ask the student to lie down, mark where his or her body ends, place his or her head at the spot where his or her feet ended.) Emphasize no gaps and no overlaps. Suggest tally marks to record the number of body lengths needed. Ask, "What if there are parts left over? What's another way you could measure in body lengths?" (e.g., Cut a piece of string equal to his or her body length.)

❏ Discuss how everyone can use his or her body length to measure longer distances. Reveal the teacher's Measure Monster. Discuss how it is constructed to equal the teacher's height. Demonstrate how to use this to measure lengths by placing the unit at the start, marking the end, then moving it end-to-end with no gaps and no overlaps. Ask, "How many Measure Monsters long is the room? Why might the number of units be different from the first body length?"

❏ Have each student work with a partner. Have them make their own body unit from a cardboard strip. Have them decorate it to look like a weird monster. Have them find three lengths to measure with their Measure Monster. Have them estimate how many units they will need first, then check with a partner.

Variation
❏ Have students record measures on the cards, or create their own challenges for another team to use.

24

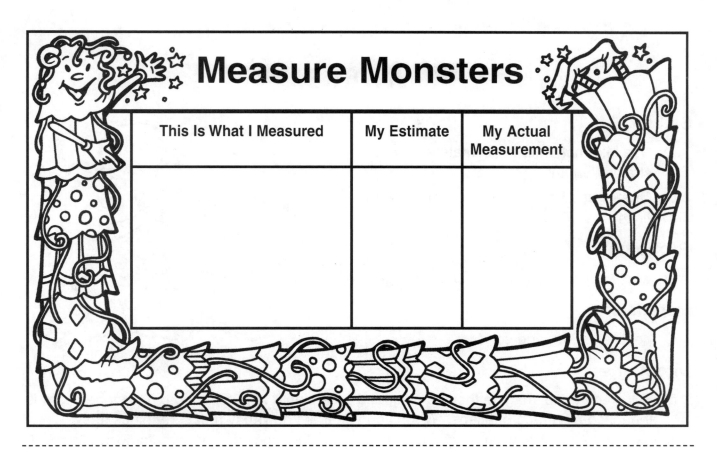

Measure Monsters

This Is What I Measured	My Estimate	My Actual Measurement

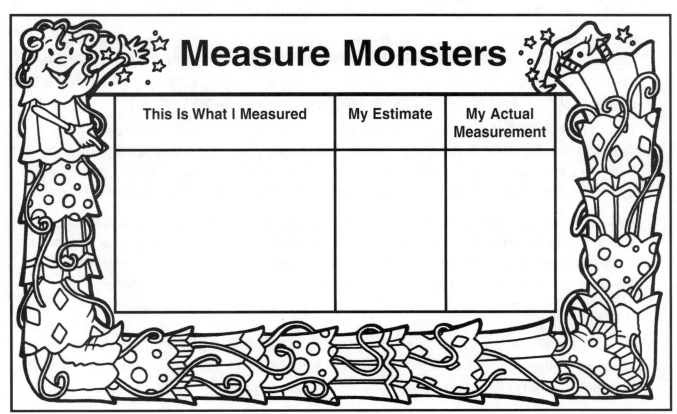

Measure Monsters

This Is What I Measured	My Estimate	My Actual Measurement

Aliens

Skills

❑ Use informal units to estimate and measure straight lengths

❑ Order three or more lengths using informal units

Grouping

❑ whole class   ❑ small groups

Materials

❑ pencils, paper, and scissors

Directions

❑ Tell students to imagine they have landed on a planet in outer space. Tell students, "It is inhabited by a race of aliens. When you ask them how they measure things, they explain to you that when they measure lengths, they measure in zurfs for long lengths, grolls for medium-size lengths, and yahoos for really small lengths."

❑ Ask students, "What's a zurf? What makes you think that?" With their team, have students decide what it looks like. Have them make a model of their zurf. Have them estimate, measure, and record at least five different lengths using their zurfs. Have them compare their measures with another team. Ask, "What do you notice?"

❑ Ask students, "What's a groll? What makes you think that?" With their team, have students decide what it looks like. Have them make a model of their groll. Have them estimate, measure, and record at least five different lengths using their grolls. Have them compare their measures with another team. Ask, "What do you notice?"

❑ Ask students, "What's a yahoo? What makes you think that?" With their team, have students decide what it looks like. Have them make a model of their yahoo. Have them estimate, measure, and record at least five different lengths using their yahoos. Have them compare their measures with another team. Ask, "What do you notice?"

Variation

❑ Tells students that when these aliens measure extremely long things, they measure in gats. Ask students, "What could these be? Why do the aliens need these? Why not just measure long things in zurfs?"

Perimeters

Skills

- ❑ Use informal units to estimate and measure curves
- ❑ Use informal units to estimate and measure perimeters
- ❑ Order three or more lengths using informal units

Grouping

- ❑ whole class   ❑ small groups   ❑ pairs

Materials

- ❑ chalk and chalkboard
- ❑ a variety of 3-D shapes (e.g., boxes, cylinders)
- ❑ informal units (e.g., toothpicks, paperclips, straws)
- ❑ perimeters worksheet (page 28)

Directions

- ❑ With students, discuss things that go all the way around the edge of something. (e.g., a fence around land, a bracelet or a watch strap around the wrist, a necklace around a neck, a label around a can)
- ❑ Ask students, "How can you measure how long these are? (e.g., Lay the necklace out in a straight line.) How can you measure them if they are fixed like a fence? (e.g., Measure and compare in strides.)" Tell students another name for these measures is *perimeter*. Tell them that a perimeter is a length that goes all the way around the edge of something.
- ❑ Demonstrate how to find the perimeter of a box or a cylinder using informal units. Discuss how students know whether their unit is suitable. (e.g., Straws are too long for measuring the perimeter of the top of a small can.)
- ❑ Have students draw three 2-D shapes on the chalkboard.

  Ask students, "How can you find out which shape has the longest perimeter?" (e.g., Compare the lengths using a suitable informal unit such as straws.)
- ❑ Have students find three objects they think have the same perimeter. Have them decide on a suitable informal unit with which to measure. (e.g., toothpicks) Have them estimate how many units they will need; then check. Have them find a way to record their discoveries.

Variation

- ❑ Use the perimeters worksheet. Have students look at each of the shapes and decide on a suitable informal unit (e.g., finger widths) to measure the perimeter. Have them estimate how many they will need; then check. Have them find at least one other object in real life that has the same measurement.

27

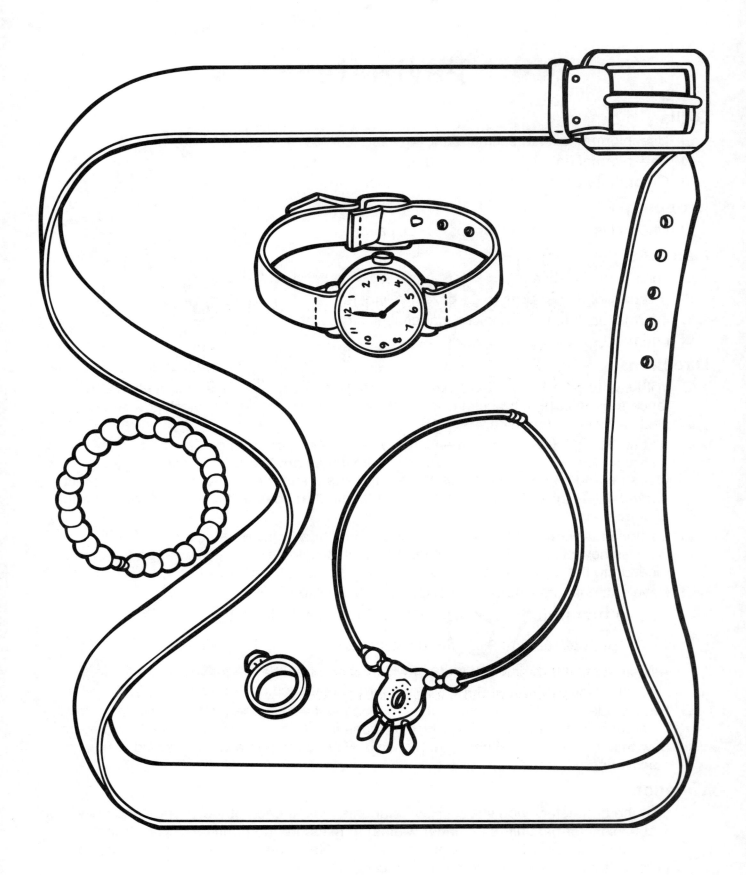

Measuring With Meters

In this unit, your students will do the following:

❏ Measure and estimate using meters

❏ Estimate and measure to the nearest half and quarter meter

❏ Order three or more lengths using meters

(The skills in this section are listed on the Skills Record Sheet on page 93.)

Strings

Skills

❏ Measure and estimate using meters

Grouping

❏ whole class   ❏ small groups   ❏ pairs

Materials

❏ Meter lengths of string for each student
❏ Meter ruler
❏ Strings worksheet (page 31)

Directions

❏ Ask everyone to close their eyes while you hand them each a piece of string. On a signal, have them stand up and open their eyes, walk around, and see what they can discover about the length of their string. (e.g., My string is as long as Lucy's string. My string is as long as five straws.)

❏ After a time limit (e.g., two minutes), discuss their discoveries together. Ask, "Did anyone discover that all the strings are the same length?" Reveal that each string is exactly one meter long. Show students the meter ruler and tell students that just about everyone around the world recognizes the meter as a suitable measure for lengths that are not too long.

❏ Have students match strings to the meter ruler.

❏ Form teams. Tell students, "In five minutes, what can your team discover about meters?" (e.g., This desk is about two meters long.) Have students select one team member to report their discoveries to the rest of the class.

Variations

❏ Have students create a class book listing objects that are about one meter long.

❏ Have students use the meter worksheet. Have them estimate how many informal units they need to match the length of their string, then check their estimate. Have students invent their own grid for another team to use.

❏ Have students take their string home. Have them find out how many cat steps, dog steps, baby crawls, etc., they need to match a meter.

How many of each unit fit along your meter string?

Object		My Estimate	Actual Measurement
	Hands		
	Feet		
	Straws		
	Toothpicks		

How many of each unit fit along your meter string?

Object		My Estimate	Actual Measurement
	Hands		
	Feet		
	Straws		
	Toothpicks		

©Teacher Created Resources, Inc.   #3532 Math in Action

Meter Monsters

Skills

❑ Measure and estimate using meters

Grouping

❑ whole class   ❑ small groups   ❑ pairs

Materials

❑ cardboard, scissors, colored paper
❑ sample Meter Monster (exactly 1 meter long)
❑ meter lengths of string
❑ meter ruler
❑ Meter Monster measures worksheet (page 33)

Directions

❑ Make a sample Meter Monster by cutting a strip of cardboard one meter long and using colored paper to decorate it to look like a monster.

❑ Discuss the advantages of everyone using the same unit for measuring. (e.g., When we measure, we should all get the same answer.)

❑ Reveal your Meter Monster. Have students estimate how many they will need to measure lengths around the classroom. (e.g., Will Sam be more than a meter tall? Is this wall shorter than six meters?) Have students check, revising starting and end points, no gaps, and no overlaps when placing your Meter Monster end to end.

❑ Have students make individual Meter Monsters. Have students check the actual lengths using the meter strings or the meter stick. They should all be exactly one meter long.

❑ Have students find three long/tall/high/wide/thick lengths to measure with their monster. Have them estimate first, then check each length in meters. Ask, "What will you do if there are bits left over or not quite enough?"

Variations

❑ Have students identify a body length that is exactly equal to one meter. (e.g., from my foot to my underarm) Have each student challenge a partner to show him or her exactly where a meter will come to on his or her body. Have students check using the teacher's Meter Monster as a measure.

❑ Have students use the Meter Monster measures worksheet. Have them find as many things as they can that are exactly a meter, a little bit more than a meter, and a little bit less than a meter.

These things are a bit less than 1 meter.

These things are exactly 1 meter long.

These things are a bit longer than 1 meter.

Flying Far

Skills

- ❏ Estimate and measure to the nearest half and quarter meter
- ❏ Order three or more lengths using meters

Grouping

- ❏ whole class   ❏ small groups   ❏ pairs

Materials

- ❏ reference book about flying objects (*optional*)
- ❏ sample paper planes
- ❏ paper, scissors, pencils, glue/stapler/tape
- ❏ meter measures (string, rulers, monsters)
- ❏ Flying High record sheet (page 35)

Directions

- ❏ Discuss types of flying objects. (e.g., a bird, helicopter, jumbo jet, balloon, kite, rocket) Ask, "What does 'a better flyer' mean?" Discuss why some objects might be better at flying than others.
- ❏ Challenge the class to design and make a paper flying object which goes the furthest distance in meters. Discuss the sample paper planes. Discuss possible construction techniques. Discuss possible test techniques.
- ❏ Have students construct their flying objects. Have them test how far they can fly. Have them experiment by attaching small objects or by rearranging the shape of their flying object in some way. Ask students, "Do heavier objects fly further? Do wider objects fly further?" Have students record flight distances in meters on their record sheet.
- ❏ Discuss advantages/disadvantages of sample class models with everyone. Ask, "Does one model stand out as the Class Champion Flyer?"

Variations

- ❏ Have students construct, test, and record flight details for other flying objects.
- ❏ Have students challenge another class to design and make a flying object that travels further than their Class Champion Flyer.

Flying Far

	Flight 1	Flight 2	Flight 3	Furthest Distance
Plane 1				
Plane 2				
Plane 3				

Flying Far

	Flight 1	Flight 2	Flight 3	Furthest Distance
Plane 1				
Plane 2				
Plane 3				

Exploring Area Language

In this unit, your students will do the following:

❑ Describe and sort surfaces using area language
(e.g., *surface area*)

(The skills in this section are listed on the Skills Record Sheet on page 93.)

Open Them Flat

Skills

❏ Describe and sort surfaces using area language.

Grouping

❏ whole class   ❏ small groups   ❏ pairs

Materials

❏ boxes, bags, or other containers that can be taken apart and laid flat

❏ Open Them Flat recording sheet (page 38)

Directions

❏ Discuss different ways to package objects.
(e.g., dog food comes in cans, cereal comes in boxes)

❏ Tell students that the outside area of something is called the *surface area*. Observe the surface area of some boxes and bags. Ask students, "How can you compare the surface area of two packages or boxes?" (e.g., take the box apart and lay it flat)

❏ Demonstrate how to cut open a box or bag until the surface area is flat and can be compared with another box or bag. Review safety issues, such as using care with scissors.

❏ Have each pair of students select two boxes or bags that they estimate to have the same surface area. Tell them to find a way to open them out flat and check their estimates.

❏ Have students record their discoveries by drawing a picture of each container before and after they opened it out flat.

Variations

❏ Have students work in groups. Give each group an Open Them Flat recording sheet and four boxes or bags. Tell students to work together to disassemble the containers, lay them flat, and compare their surface areas. In the Container column of the recording sheet, they should draw each container as it looked when assembled, and in the Surface Area column, they should draw the container as it looks disassembled and laid flat. They can then circle the container with the largest surface area.

❏ Sort a collection of objects from the smallest to the largest surface areas.

Recording Sheet

Container	Surface Area

©*Teacher Created Resources, Inc.*

Comparing Areas

In this unit, your students will do the following:

- ❏ Reconize and construct open/closed lines
- ❏ Compare the size of two areas
- ❏ Order three or more areas

(The skills in this section are listed on the Skills Record Sheet on page 93.)

Fences

Skills

❑ Recognize and construct open/closed lines

Grouping

❑ pairs   ❑ small groups

Materials

❑ craft sticks
❑ construction materials (e.g., craft sticks, building bricks)
❑ plastic farm/zoo animals
❑ Fences worksheet (page 40)

Directions

❑ Have students describe fences in their neighborhoods. Ask, "From what are they made? For what are they used? (e.g., to keep out animals or to show where your land ends and a neighbor's land starts) Why do they have gates? (e.g., to let people go in or out)" Tell them a fence is open when the gate is open, and closed when the gate is closed.

❑ Discuss the amount of land enclosed by a fence. Ask students, "Is the space where you live large? Small? Who lives in the largest area?"

❑ Explore the idea of inside and outside. Ask students, "How do we know whether we are in or out?" Talk about what happens in the classroom if they keep the door shut. (e.g., The walls of the room are like a fence; the door is like a gate. It defines an area within a boundary.)

❑ Discuss farm animals and the enclosures they live in, compared to wild animals. Tell students fences are the boundaries to areas they can move into or out of on the farm.

❑ Have students build fenced enclosures (e.g., with craftsticks or building bricks) for toy farm animals. Ask, "Which animals have the largest area? Do any animals have about the same area?"

Variations

❑ Have each student challenge a partner to design and make fences according to his or her specifications. (e.g., an area large enough to hold 10 horses)

❑ Have students use the Fences worksheet. Have them draw a fence around all the pigs and draw another fence around all the horses. Ask, "Which area is larger? On another copy, have students draw an area to hold the chickens and pigs. Have them draw another area for the horses and sheep. Ask, "Are both areas the same size?" Have students make up their own fence instructions about area.

Which Covers More?

Skills

- ❑ Compare the sizes of two areas
- ❑ Order three or more areas

Grouping

- ❑ whole class ❑ small groups ❑ pairs

Materials

- ❑ different-shaped cloths (towels, wash cloths, etc.)
- ❑ a piece of paper and a book
- ❑ two apples
- ❑ Which Covers More? activity cards (page 43)

Directions

- ❑ Ask students, "How many different large areas do you know about at school?" (e.g., outdoor playing areas, sidewalk areas, out-of-bounds areas) Have students think of just two areas. Ask, "Which area is larger? What makes you think this?" (e.g., I imagined overlapping one on top of the other.)
- ❑ Ask students, "How can you compare two similar size areas?" Show students the different sized cloths. Ask, "How can we find out which area is larger?" (e.g., If they look about the same size, I can place one on top of the other and see if one is larger.)
- ❑ Ask students, "What's another way to compare areas?" Show students the piece of paper and the book cover. Ask, "How can we find out which area is larger?" (e.g., I can cut the paper up and rearrange it on top of the book to see if it covers the same area.)
- ❑ Ask students, "How can you compare two areas if they are not flat?" Show students two apples. Ask, "How can we find out which area is larger?" (e.g., I can peel them and compare the area covered by peel. Or I can wrap a piece of paper around one and then see if I need a larger piece to wrap the other one.)
- ❑ With a partner, have each student find pairs of objects that he or she thinks:
  a) both cover the same area
  b) have one area smaller or larger than the other
- ❑ Have students estimate first, and then check by imagining/overlapping/cutting/wrapping. Have them record their favorite discoveries.
- ❑ Discuss problems together. (e.g., What do you do/say if there is just a small difference in area? What strategy did you use to check areas that couldn't be picked up and compared directly?)

Variation

- ❑ Have students use the Which Covers More? cards and then have them invent even more challenges for another team to try.

Which Covers More?

Your hand or your foot print?

Estimate first, then find a way to check.

Who has the largest hand and foot area in your group?

Which Covers More?

Your body outline or your friend's outline?

Estimate first, then find a way to check.

Who has the smallest body outline in your group?

#3532 Math in Action

Shadows

Skills

- ❑ Compare the size of two areas
- ❑ Order three or more areas

Grouping

- ❑ whole class
- ❑ small groups

Materials

- ❑ chalk
- ❑ Shadows recording sheet (page 45)

Directions

- ❑ Ask students, "What are shadows? What do you think makes a shadow appear?"
- ❑ Take students outdoors. Demonstrate how they can trace around a shadow with chalk. Shadow areas can then be compared.
- ❑ Have students find objects that cast very small shadow areas. Ask, "What's the smallest you can discover?"
- ❑ Have students find objects that cast very large shadow areas. Ask, "What's the largest you can discover?"
- ❑ Have students work in teams outside. Have them create one giant shadow monster from the combined shadows of their team. Ask, "Which team can create the largest shadow monster? How does the time of day affect the size of your shadow monsters?"
- ❑ Have students record their discoveries. Have them circle the smallest shadow they recorded. Have them put an X under the largest area recorded.

Variation

- ❑ Ask students, "How much floor space does your cat or dog take up when they are sleeping?" Have them find a way to trace around their body outline. Have them compare areas. Ask, "Which pet takes up the most area? Do they always take up the same area when sleeping? Which pet takes up the least area?"

Small Areas

Medium Areas

Large Areas

Using Informal Area Units

In this unit, your students will do the following:

❏ Use informal units to estimate and measure areas

❏ Order three or more areas using informal units

(The skills in this section are listed on the Skills Record Sheet on page 93.)

Cover It

Skills

❏ Use informal units to estimate and measure areas

Grouping

❏ whole class   ❏ small groups

Materials

❏ class mat or rug

❏ various flat objects to use as informal units (e.g., counters, plastic bread ties, lids, shells, washcloths, envelopes, sheets of paper, blocks, newspaper pages, bath towels)

Directions

❏ Ask students, "How many students can sit on the class mat?" Have students estimate first, then check. Ask, "Can you fit more students if everybody stands? Why/why not?"

❏ Tell students that when they compare areas, they can use a smaller area as a unit. Ask, "How many of the smaller areas cover the larger area? How can this method help us?" (e.g., We can now compare areas easily by counting the units needed to cover each area.)

❏ Ask students, "What can you use to measure small areas?" (e.g., bread ties, counters, shells) Demonstrate by covering some small areas. Have students estimate how many units they need before measuring.

❏ Ask students, "What can you use to measure medium size areas?" (e.g., handprints, footprints, books) Demonstrate by covering some medium areas. Have students estimate how many units they need before measuring.

❏ Ask students, "What can you use to measure large areas?" (e.g., body outlines, newspaper pages, bath towels) Demonstrate by covering some large areas. Have students estimate how many units they need before measuring.

❏ Have students find small, medium, and large areas to measure and compare. Have them decide which unit is best to use for each area.

❏ Discuss problems with units they selected. (e.g., Were there any gaps or overlaps? Did some units cover areas more easily than others? Why?)

❏ Have students record their favorite discoveries.

Rearrange It

Skills

- ❑ Use informal units to estimate and measure areas
- ❑ Order three or more areas using informal units

Grouping

- ❑ whole class   ❑ small groups

Materials

- ❑ various geometric tiles
- ❑ pencils and paper
- ❑ geometric shaped cookies
- ❑ Rearrange It shapes (pages 49 and 50, preferably on cardboard)
- ❑ Rearrange It puzzle cards (page 51)

Directions

- ❑ Demonstrate how to fit some geometric tiles together and trace around them on paper to create the outline of a large shape.
- ❑ Discuss how students can now use this as a puzzle by asking a friend to look at their outline and then estimate how many tiles they need to cover the whole picture.
- ❑ Have students explore further by tracing tiles, exchanging tracings, estimating, and rearranging tiles to check their estimates.

Variations

- ❑ Repeat the above activities, but use geometric shaped cookies in place of tiles, or make cookie shapes with a cookie cutter and play clay.
- ❑ Have students cut out one set of Rearrange It shapes. Ask, "How many different new shapes can you discover by rearranging these pieces?" Have them trace these onto paper as one large outline puzzle for a friend to try.
- ❑ Have students try the activities on the Rearrange It puzzle cards.

Answers:

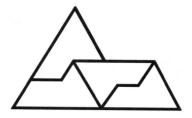
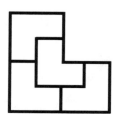
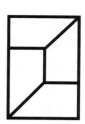
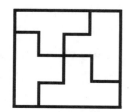

Pentagons

- -

L Shapes

Trapezium

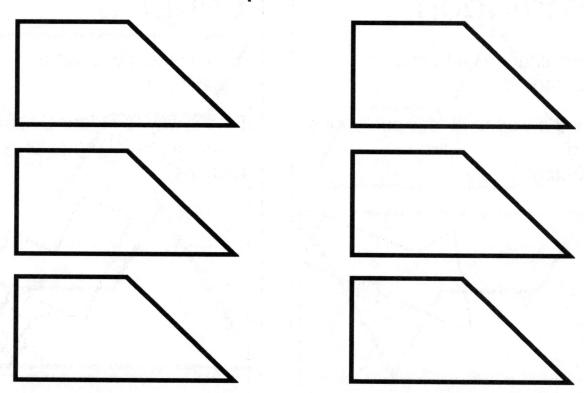

T Shapes

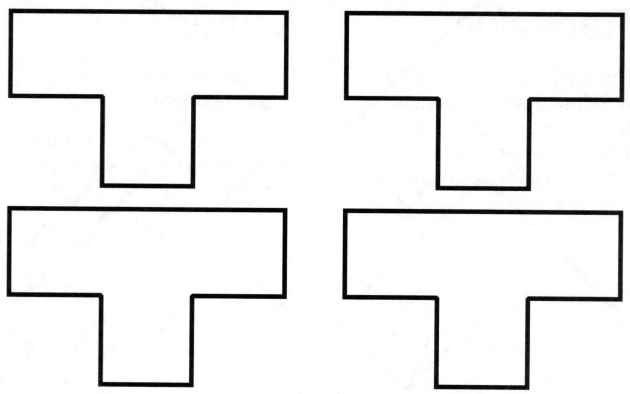

Pentagon

This shape is an unusual pentagon.

Find a way to fit four pentagons together to make one larger pentagon.

Letter L

This shape looks like a squashed L.

Find a way to fit four L-shapes together to make one larger L-shape.

Trapezium

This shape is a trapezium. It looks like a square stretched on one corner. Find a way to fit four trapeziums together to make one large rectangle.

Letter T

This shape looks like a squashed letter T.

Find a way to fit four T-shapes together to make one large square.

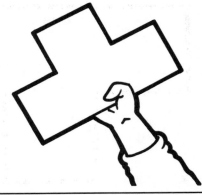

Exploring Volume Language

In this unit, your students will do the following:

- ❏ Observe and discuss the space occupied by objects
- ❏ Pack a variety of objects into defined spaces
- ❏ Use volume and capacity language, (e.g., *pack, fill, empty*)

(The skills in this section are listed on the Skills Record Sheet on page 94.)

How Large Is It?

Skills

❑ Observe and discuss the space occupied by objects

Grouping

❑ whole class

Materials

❑ balloons

❑ blindfold

❑ variety of 3-D objects (e.g., box, ball, book)

❑ paper and pencils

❑ animal face parts (page 54), scissors, glue

Directions

❑ Discuss the size of objects around students. Ask them, "What's the largest thing you can see? What does large mean?" (e.g., the space taken up by an object) "What do you think is the largest thing in the world? What is the smallest thing?"

❑ Blow up a balloon. Discuss the idea that large things can also be hollow. Ask students, "What can you see that is about as large as this balloon? Is it hollow also? Does the size depend on whether it is hollow or not?"

❑ Blindfold a student. Ask him or her to feel a variety of objects. Can he or she identify whether each object feels large or small or even the same size as another object? How can he or she tell? (e.g., Is this as large as Minh's backpack?)

❑ Have students predict the size of objects using their hands. (e.g., Show the size of Sam's lunchbox.) Have them check size estimates wherever possible by comparing with the real objects.

❑ Have students draw pictures of some very large and very small objects. Have them compare, discuss, and display.

Variations

❑ Have students blow up balloons to make animal heads. Discuss and compare the different sizes. Have them decorate with cut-out animal face parts. Display.

❑ Create a class book about the size of objects. Cut out magazine pictures and add drawings and comments from students.

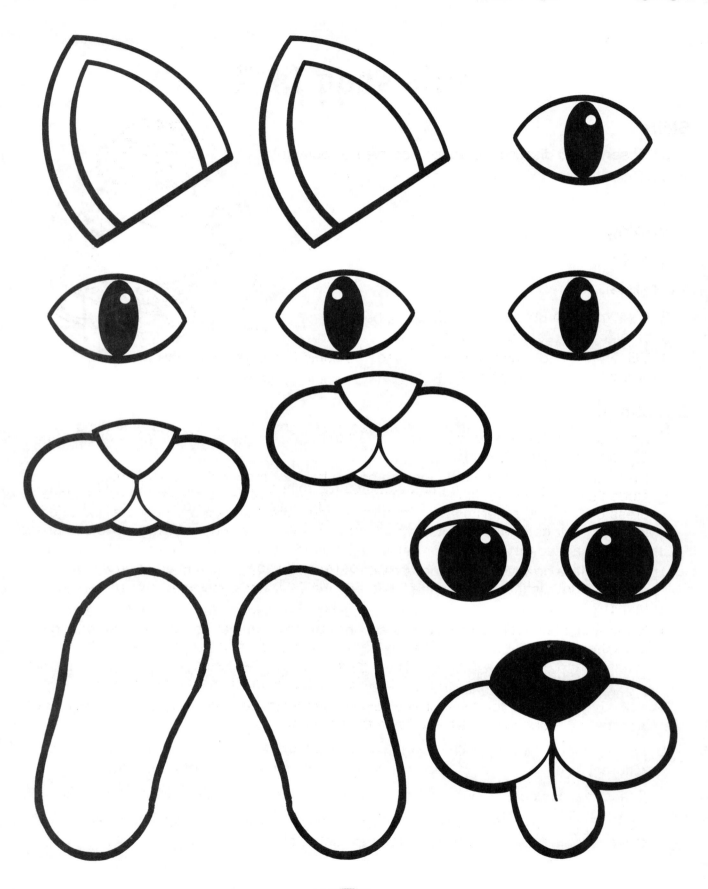

Will They Fit?

Skills

- ❑ Observe and discuss the space occupied by objects
- ❑ Pack a variety of objects into defined spaces
- ❑ Use volume and capacity language

Grouping

- ❑ whole class

Materials

- ❑ a very large shoe
- ❑ small box and some oranges
- ❑ Will They Fit? discussion cards A (page 56 copied onto yellow paper)
- ❑ Will They Fit? discussion cards B (page 57 copied onto blue paper)

Directions

- ❑ Ask students, "What size foot do you need to fit into this shoe? How many of your feet do you think could fit inside it?"
- ❑ Discuss the fact that some things can be too large or too small to be a perfect fit. Have students identify some things that they know are a good fit. (e.g., a hand and a glove, a dress on their big sister) Have students tell you some things they know are not a good fit. (e.g., Our garage is built for two cars but we own only one car. There is lots of space left over.)
- ❑ Demonstrate how to pack oranges neatly into a box. Ask, "How many do you guess will fit inside? Is there any space left over?" (e.g., I guess you need six oranges to fill that box.)
- ❑ Have students shuffle both sets of cards and place them into two separate piles. Then have them turn over and read the top card in each pile. Tell them to imagine the situation and discuss it together. Have them estimate the size of the item on each card. Ask, "Will they fit together?" (e.g., Could eight grandmas fit inside the teacher's car?)
- ❑ Ask students, "Can you think of any special circumstance when they will fit?" (e.g., four whales and a shopping cart—perhaps they are only toy whales)

Variations

- ❑ Have students create their own set of Will They Fit? discussion cards for another class to discuss.
- ❑ Have students use the Will They Fit? activity cards. Have them explore different ways to make a container with an exact fit for each set of objects.

your feet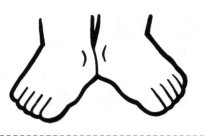

2 cats

3 cars

4 whales

8 grandmas

10 students

15 cans

20 fish

50 beetles

100 people

a jar

your dad's shoes

a
cardboard box

a medium-size
aquarium

a
shopping cart

your
teacher's car

your
garage

a
swimming pool

your
living room

an
airplane

Comparing Volumes

In this unit, your students will do the following:

❏ Compare and describe two or more volumes and capacities

❏ Identify objects with the same volume and capacity

❏ Understand that objects with the same volume and capacity may have different shapes

(The skills in this section are listed on the Skills Record Sheet on page 94.)

Which Is Larger?

Skills

❑ Compare and describe two or more volumes and capacities

Grouping

❑ whole class   ❑ pairs

Materials

❑ objects around the classroom
❑ Which Is Larger? label cards (page 60)
❑ paper and pencils
❑ Which Is Larger? discussion cards (page 61)

Directions

❑ Ask students, "What's the largest thing in this room? How do you know? What's the smallest thing you can see in this room?"

❑ Hold up two objects at random. Ask students, "Which one is larger? What clues do you use to judge size? How do you know just by looking?" Discuss ideas together.

❑ Discuss the five Which Is Larger? label cards. Demonstrate how to place objects on either side of each label to record their decisions.

takes up much more space than

❑ Have students walk around with a partner and find pairs of objects to label. Have them record two of their favorites on paper.

❑ For a class challenge, have students name two objects. (e.g., a giraffe and a hippo) Ask, "Which one is larger?" Have them compare pairs of objects which are quite different in size, as well as objects that are very similar in size.

Variations

❑ Have students shuffle the Which Is Larger? discussion cards. Have them select any two cards. Tell them to think about how large each object might be in real life. Ask, "Which of the two objects would be larger?" Have students consider different possibilities. (e.g., a golf ball is small but a beach ball can be very large)

❑ Have students invent 10 more discussion cards for another team to try.

59

takes up much more space than

takes up a little more space than

takes up about the same space as

takes up a little less space than

takes up much less space than

Discussion Cards

a box of soap	a television set
a pumpkin	a carton of milk
a puppy	a ball
a rooster	a rock
cat	a baby

#3532 Math in Action

Find a Pair

Skills

❑ Identify objects with the same volume and capacity

❑ Understand that objects with the same volume
or capacity may have different shapes

Grouping

❑ pairs   ❑ small groups

Materials

❑ various containers—milk cartons, boxes, bottles, cans

❑ water, rice, marbles, small blocks

❑ scissors, glue, tape, play clay

❑ Find a Pair activity cards (page 63)

❑ ½ cup and 1 cup measuring cups

Directions

❑ Ask students, "Do all things that hold the same amount have to be the same shape?"
Discuss different views together.

❑ Demonstrate how a full milk carton of water can be poured into a second, identical
carton to exactly the same level. Tell students to notice that they are the same shape
and hold the same amount of water.

❑ Ask students, "What if the container was a different shape? Can you find another
container that holds exactly the same amount of water as the milk carton?" Have
students check and then discuss their results together.

❑ Demonstrate how to make a small container from play clay. Fill it with water. Make a
second container that is a different shape. (e.g., it is longer and narrower) Have
students check the size by pouring the water from one container to another.

❑ Have students work with a partner. Have them find pairs of containers that hold about
the same amount of material (e.g., rice, marbles, small blocks) as each other but have a
different shape.

❑ Discuss some of the solution strategies together. (e.g., I cut down this container until it
held the same amount of rice as that one.)

Variation

❑ Ask students, "How can you make your own containers?" (e.g., Cut up boxes or bottles.)
Have students use the Find a Pair activity cards. Have them compare and discuss the
different shapes they discover or make. Have them look at the size of each one in their
pair. Ask, "What do you notice?"

Find or make two containers that hold the same amount of marbles but are different shapes. Next, find a container that holds exactly five marbles.

Find or make two containers that hold the same amount of blocks but are different shapes. Next, find a container that holds exactly 10 blocks.

Find or make two containers that hold the same amount of rice but are different shapes. Next, find a container that holds exactly one cup of rice.

Find or make two containers that hold the same amount of water but are different shapes. Next, find a container that holds exactly half a cup of water.

Using Informal Volume Units

In this unit, your students will do the following:

- ❏ Fill and empty containers using a variety of materials
- ❏ Use informal units to estimate and measure volume and capacity
- ❏ Record volume and capacity measurements using tallying

(The skills in this section are listed on the Skills Record Sheet on page 94.)

How Many?

Skills

❑ Fill and empty containers using a variety of materials
❑ Use informal units to estimate and measure volume and capacity
❑ Record volume and capacity measurements using tallying

Grouping

❑ whole class
❑ small groups

Materials

❑ water, cups, containers
❑ packing materials (e.g., blocks, marbles, books)
❑ How Many? discussion/activity cards (page 66)
❑ paper and pencils
❑ materials for activity cards

Directions

❑ Ask students, "Why would you need to know which of two or more containers is the larger?" (e.g., to hold the most drink for a picnic lunch)

❑ Ask students, "How do we know which container holds the most?" Discuss suggestions for comparing two containers. (e.g., I can tell by looking that this one is larger.)

❑ Ask students, "What if the two containers look similar?" Discuss the idea of counting up how many smaller containers they need to fill each of the containers. Demonstrate by filling one of the containers with cups of water. Ask, "How will you keep count?" (e.g., Make tally marks on paper.) Ask, "How many cups do you need to fill the second container?" Have students estimate and then check. Have them compare tally counts.

❑ Ask students, "What else can we measure this way?" (e.g., How many oranges will fill a bag? How many buckets of water will fill a bath? How many people will fill a car?)

❑ Have students work in small groups. Have them explore the How Many? cards. Have them collect the equipment they need. Have them estimate how many of each unit they will use. They should discuss with their partners at least two ways to check. Have students find another container that holds the same amount. Have them record some of their discoveries. Have students make up more questions to explore.

❑ Discuss discoveries and any problems together.

Variation

❑ At home, have students answer questions such as "How many cans fit in a cupboard? How many towels? How many saucepans?" Have them look for items around their home that they can count. Have them compare their results with friends back at school.

How many cups of water in a saucepan?

How many marbles in a bag?

How many blocks in a box?

How many books in a backpack?

How many cups of water in a teapot?

How many cans of water in a bucket?

How many lunch boxes in a basket?

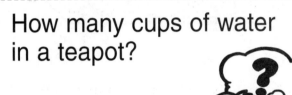

How many spoons of rice in a cup?

How many pencils in a pencil case?

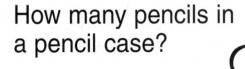

How many cotton swabs in a box?

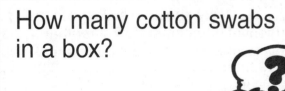

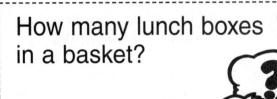

Groceries

Skills

- ❏ Use informal units to estimate and measure volume and capacity
- ❏ Record volume and capacity measurements using tallying

Grouping

- ❏ whole class ❏ small groups ❏ pairs

Materials

- ❏ grocery items (e.g., cans, boxes, tubes)
- ❏ empty boxes, crates, shopping bags
- ❏ paper and pencils
- ❏ Groceries Discussion Cards (page 68)

Directions

- ❏ Ask students, "Why do you need shopping bags?" (e.g., to help carry things to the car without spilling them everywhere)
- ❏ Ask students, "How many groceries can you fit inside a shopping bag?" Discuss different possibilities. Ask, "What if all the items were the same such as cans of cat food? How many cans do you estimate would fit inside?"
- ❏ Ask students, "What if you need to know how many cans would fit altogether, yet you only have one can?" (e.g., Estimate the space one can takes up and keep mentally adding spaces until you've "filled" the whole bag.)
- ❏ Have students explore stacking and packing in groups. Have them investigate how many of each item they would need to fill a crate, a bag, or a box. Ask, "Are some items easier to pack than others? What about how heavy they feel? Can you still carry them safely even though they fill the container?"
- ❏ Have students record some of their discoveries.

Variations

- ❏ Have students shuffle the discussion cards. Have them read the top card and discuss the size and shape of the container they would need to hold this set of grocery items. Have them demonstrate with their hands. Discuss different possibilities. Have students justify why they selected this size and shape.
- ❏ Ask students, "What size container would you need to hold four dogs? Three kittens? Ten mice? Discuss. Have students demonstrate with their hands.

Discussion Cards

15 tubes
of toothpaste

10 packages
of cookies

3 boxes of
detergent

20 cans
of soup

2 bags
of chips

8 soda bottles

5 packages
of cheese

18 yogurt
containers

4 apple
pies

13 loaves
of bread

Exploring Displacement

In this unit, your students will do the following:

❏ Compare volumes by water displacement (rising levels)

❏ Compare volumes by water displacement (overflow)

❏ Compare volumes by water displacement (falling levels)

❏ Understand that volumes stay the same when broken into smaller parts

(The skills in this section are listed on the Skills Record Sheet on page 94.)

Drop It In

Skills

- ❏ Compare volumes by water displacement (rising levels)
- ❏ Compare volumes by water displacement (overflow)
- ❏ Understand volumes stay the same when broken into smaller parts

Grouping

- ❏ whole class ❏ small groups

Materials

- ❏ clear containers, water, objects, overflow trays or bowls, marker pens
- ❏ interlocking blocks (e.g., building bricks), play clay
- ❏ Drop It In activity cards (page 71)

Directions

- ❏ Ask students, "When you have a bath, how do you know how much water to put in?" (e.g., just enough to cover your body) "What happens to the water level when you get in completely?" (e.g., It goes up.) "What happens to the water level when you get out of the bath?" (e.g., It goes down again.)
- ❏ Tell students to imagine they have a new aquarium full of water. Ask, "What will happen if you put in one large fish? To where should you fill it so the water doesn't spill over?"
- ❏ Ask students, "What else do we use in our daily lives that involves water this way?" (e.g., adding ice cubes to a drink, adding potatoes to a pot of water)
- ❏ Form small groups with an activity card for each group. Find the equipment they need. Have students explore different ways to solve their problem. Tell students to think of extra activities on the same topic.
- ❏ Discuss problems. (e.g., How many different ways can you place an object into the water? With a piece of string tied around it . . . just by pressing down with their fingers)
- ❏ Discuss discoveries. (e.g., How does the overflow method help us measure size? For example, they can measure the amount of water in the overflow tray—the largest object spills the most water.)

Variation

- ❏ Have students explore ways to compare the size of large objects (e.g., balloons) using bins or large buckets of water.

Drop It In ①

Find three waterproof objects that you think are close in size. Estimate which one is the largest.

Partly fill a clear container with water.

Mark the water level. Predict what will happen when you drop an object in and then remove it.

How can you use this to measure size?

From the results, place your objects in order by size.

Check your estimate.

Drop It In ②

Find three objects that you think are close in size. Estimate which one is the largest.

Place a small bucket in a larger empty bowl. Fill the bucket to the brim with water. Predict what will happen when you place an object in the bucket.

How can you use this to measure size?

From the results, place the objects in order by size.

Check your estimate.

Take It Out

Skills

❏ Compare volumes by water displacement (falling levels)

Grouping

❏ whole class   ❏ small groups

Materials

❏ a box of cornflakes, a bottle of juice

❏ clear containers, water, objects, marker pens

❏ Take It Out activity cards (page 73)

❏ materials for activity cards

Directions

❏ Tell students to imagine they are setting up a small aquarium. They arrange some rocks in the bottom and fill it up with water. Ask them, "What will happen to the water level if you decide to remove the rocks?"

❏ Tell students to imagine they are given a large gift-wrapped box as a birthday present. When they open it up, it is full of shredded paper with their present hidden in the middle. Ask them, "What happens when you remove your present?" (e.g., The height of the paper goes down to fill the space where the present was.)

❏ Tell students to imagine they have a new box of cornflakes. They decide to eat a cupful for breakfast. Ask them, "What happens to the height of the cornflakes in the box when you remove a cupful?" Have students estimate first, then check how many cupfuls there are in one box.

❏ Tell students to imagine they are planning a party. They need enough juice for 10 people. Ask them, "How many people would one bottle serve? How many bottles will you need to buy?" Have students estimate first, then find a way to check. (e.g., pour a cupful for each person)

❏ Form small groups with an activity card for each group. Discuss activities briefly. Find the equipment they need. Remember to select objects that can get wet without any damage. Have students explore different ways to solve their problem. Tell them to think of extra activities on the same topic.

❏ Discuss problems and discoveries.

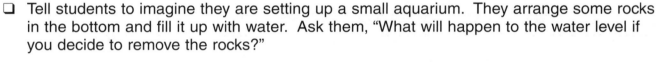

Take It Out ①

You need a full container of rice and a cup. Guess how many cups of rice there are altogether.

Predict what the new level will be when you pour out one cup of rice.

Pour out one cup of rice.

Keep predicting and pouring until the container is empty.

Do your estimates get more accurate?

Try this again with different-shaped containers.

Take It Out ②

You need a cup and a full bottle of water.

Predict what the new level will be when you pour out one cup of water.

Pour out one cup of water.

Keep predicting and pouring until the bottle is empty.

Do your estimates get more accurate?

Try this again with different-shaped bottles.

#3532 Math in Action

Exploring Mass Language

In this unit, your students will do the following:

- ❏ Use mass language (e.g., *heavy, light*)
- ❏ Lift to compare two or more masses
- ❏ Understand that size is not always related to mass

(The skills in this section are listed on the Skills Record Sheet on page 94.)

Is It Heavier?

Skills

- ❑ Use mass language (e.g., *heavy, light*)
- ❑ Lift to compare two or more masses
- ❑ Understand that size is not always related to mass

Grouping

- ❑ whole class ❑ small groups

Materials

- ❑ a collection of objects (with obviously different masses) for each group
- ❑ an ice-cream container with a lid, a collection of smaller objects that can each fit inside
- ❑ Is It Heavier? activity cards (page 76)
- ❑ Is It Heavier? discussion cards (page 77)

Directions

- ❑ Ask students, "How accurate are you at estimating heaviness? Ask a friend to place five objects on a table. Without touching these objects, tell your partner how to put the objects into order by heaviness."
- ❑ Ask students, "How can you check your guesses? (e.g., Place an object in each hand and say which feels heavier.) Does closing your eyes make it any easier? Does exchanging the objects from one hand to another?"
- ❑ Discuss the idea that lifting the objects is only a rough way to check. Sometimes the differences are so small it is difficult for our hands to feel the difference.
- ❑ Form small groups with an activity card for each group. Collect the equipment they need.
- ❑ Discuss problems and discoveries.
- ❑ Pass around five different objects for everyone to feel. Ask, "Which object is the heaviest? The lightest?" Secretly place one of these objects into a container and put the lid on. Have students pass the container around the group. Ask, "Can everyone guess what is inside just by feeling how heavy it is?"

Variations

- ❑ Have students shuffle the discussion cards. Have them turn over the top two cards. Discuss how heavy each object might feel. Ask, "Which one is the heavier of the two?" Have students try to find different possibilities.
- ❑ Have students sort three or more discussion cards into order by heaviness. Have students make up their own set of Is It Heavier? discussion cards.

Is It Heavier?

Select an interesting toy.

Feel how heavy it is. Without touching them, select objects you think are heavier than this toy.

Then select objects you think are lighter than this toy.

Find a way to check your guesses.

Try this again with another toy.

Is It Heavier? ②

Point to two objects that you think are as heavy as each other.

Check your guesses.

Can you find two objects that are as heavy as each other but one is much larger?

Discussion Cards

a brick	a kitten
a bottle of juice	a baby giraffe
a bed	a cow
an apple	a bunch of celery
a space alien	a bicycle

Does Large Mean Heavy?

Skills

❑ Lift to compare two or more masses

❑ Understand that size is not always related to mass

Grouping

❑ whole class

❑ small groups

Materials

❑ a balloon, a beach ball, a golf ball

❑ paper and pencils

❑ Does Large Mean Heavy? activity cards (page 79) and corresponding materials

Directions

❑ Ask students, "Which is heavier—a beach ball or a golf ball? Why?"

❑ Blow up the balloon until it is as large as possible. Ask students, "Which of the three objects is the heaviest now? Which object is the largest? Does a large size always mean heavy? Why?"

❑ Challenge the class to find objects from around the room that are large but light.

❑ Pass the objects around so that students can feel and compare them. Ask them, "Who has the largest object? Who has the lightest object?"

❑ Challenge everyone to now find an object from around the room that is small but heavy.

❑ Pass the objects around so that students can feel and compare them. Ask them, "Who has the smallest object? Who has the heaviest object?"

❑ Discuss their results together.

❑ Have students record their favorite discoveries.

Variations

❑ Have students work in small groups or pairs with a Does Large Mean Heavy? activity card each. Have them collect the equipment they need. Discuss their results and compare objects together.

❑ Have students make a class display or book about their results. Challenge everyone to add changes to the book as a new item that fits the criteria is discovered. Have students collect examples from around the home, too.

What's the largest object you can discover that feels as heavy as a calculator?

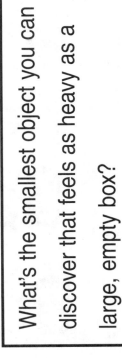

What's the smallest object you can discover that feels as heavy as a large, empty box?

What's the largest object you can discover that feels lighter than a shoe?

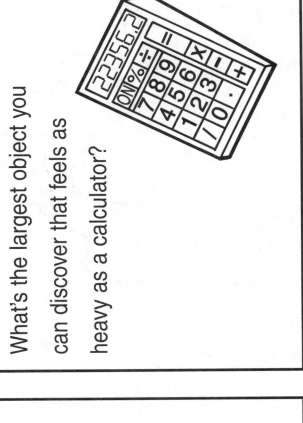

What's the smallest object you can discover that feels heavier than a book?

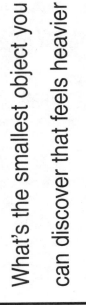

Using a Balance

In this unit, your students will do the following:

❏ Use an equal-arm balance to compare masses

❏ Predict and interpret actions of an equal-arm balance

❏ Order three or more masses by lifting; check using a balance

(The skills in this section are listed on the Skills Record Sheet on page 94.)

Make a Balance

Skills

- ❏ Use an equal-arm balance to compare masses
- ❏ Predict and interpret actions of an equal-arm balance
- ❏ Order three or more masses by lifting; check using a balance

Grouping

- ❏ whole class   ❏ small groups

Materials

- ❏ dowel, rulers, coat hangers, buckets, ice-cream/yogurt tubs, paper/foam cups, string, cotton, scissors
- ❏ pan, bucket, and balance scales
- ❏ Make a Balance examples (page 82)
- ❏ Make a Balance activity cards (page 83)

Directions

- ❏ Ask students, "What does it mean when you say something balances? What uses this idea?" (e.g., circus performers, someone riding a bicycle)
- ❏ Discuss the pan, bucket, and balance scales. Ask students, "What can you do with one of these? Where do you find them in daily life?" (e.g., in a grocery store or fruit stand)
- ❏ Ask students, "What are other ways to make a balance?" Discuss suggestions.
- ❏ Form small groups. Challenge each group to design and make their own balance. The sample cards show two different ideas.
- ❏ Have students explore what happens if they rearrange items on their balance. (e.g., move one pan closer to the center, add extra masses on one side)
- ❏ Ask students, "How can you test each balance for accuracy?" (e.g., Place identical objects in either side and watch what happens.)

Variations

- ❏ Use the activity cards in small groups.
- ❏ Have students make a list or a class book about uses of mass measurers in daily life. (e.g., kitchen scales, bathroom scales, spring balances)

#3532 Math in Action

Bucket Balance

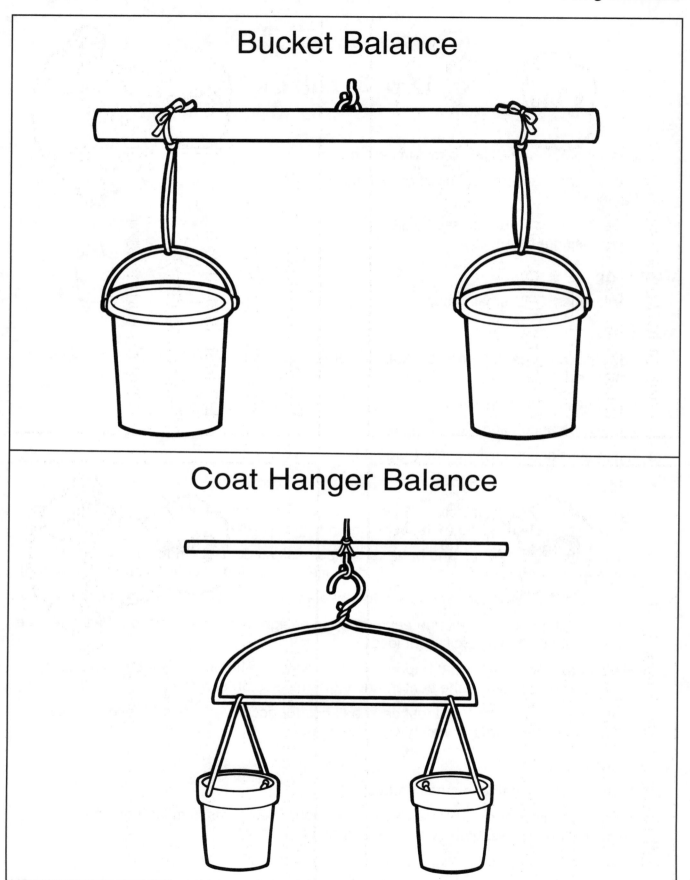

Coat Hanger Balance

Look at two objects on a balance. Say which object is heavier. Check by lifting. What do you notice?

Put three or more objects into order by heaviness. Lift first, then use a balance to check. What do you notice?

Lift two objects. Predict, then check, what will happen to each side when you place them on a balance. What do you notice?

Lift objects to find two which you think have the same mass. Check with a balance. What do you notice?

What Balances It?

Skills

- ❑ Use an equal-arm balance to compare masses
- ❑ Predict and interpret actions of an equal-arm balance

Grouping

- ❑ whole class
- ❑ small groups

Materials

- ❑ balances
- ❑ collections of light to heavy objects
- ❑ containers of informal mass units
- ❑ paper and pencils
- ❑ What Balances It? activity cards (page 85)

Directions

- ❑ Ask students, "How do you know if two things balance each other?"
- ❑ Review how to test an empty balance for accuracy. Demonstrate how to make the two sides equal. (e.g., pull one bucket closer to the center.)
- ❑ Have students find two objects they think have the same mass. (e.g., a toy and a book) Have them predict and then check what happens to each side when they use a balance.
- ❑ Ask students, "What lighter objects balance one of these objects?" (e.g., How many bolts balance the toy? How many shells?") Have them guess first and then check.
- ❑ Ask students, "What if you have four pine cones in one side? What will balance these?" Have students guess first and then check. (e.g., 14 pencils)
- ❑ Form small groups with an activity card for each group. Check their balances for accuracy.
- ❑ Rotate activities after a time limit.
- ❑ Have students record their favorite discoveries.

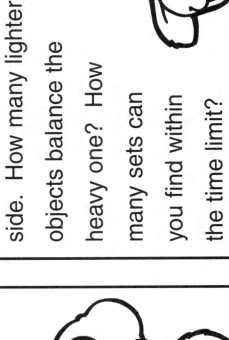

Place a heavy object on one side. How many lighter objects balance the heavy one? How many sets can you find within the time limit?

Balance sets of heavy objects. If there are three on one side, how many on the other? If there are four on one side, how many on the other?

Find two objects that balance each other. How many pairs can you find within the time limit?

Find different things to balance one thing. (e.g., one stapler balanced by 40 blocks or a small book) How many can you find within the time limit?

#3532 Math in Action

Using Informal Mass Units

In this unit, your students will do the following:

- ❏ Use informal units to estimate and measure mass
- ❏ Select an appropriate informal unit to measure mass
- ❏ Record mass measurements using tallying
- ❏ Solve problems using mass concepts
- ❏ Work cooperatively in a team

(The skills in this section are listed on the Skills Record Sheet on page 94.)

Balance It

Skills

- ❏ Use informal units to estimate and measure mass
- ❏ Select an appropriate informal unit to measure mass
- ❏ Record mass measurements using tallying

Grouping

- ❏ pairs

Materials

- ❏ a balance
- ❏ a small toy
- ❏ counters
- ❏ dice

Directions

- ❏ Ask students, "How do you know when something feels as heavy as another thing? How can you check?" (e.g., You can lift, then check using a balance.)
- ❏ Ask students, "How heavy does this toy feel?" (e.g., lighter than that book, heavier than a pair of scissors) "How heavy is a handful of counters?" Have students estimate how many counters they will need to balance the toy.
- ❏ Review how to check a balance for accuracy.
- ❏ Have students place the toy in one side of the balance.
- ❏ In turn, have students throw the dice, add the numbers on their dice, and place a matching number of counters into the other pan. Have them count and record by tallying the number of counters used.
- ❏ The winner is the player whose counters finally balance the toy.
- ❏ Ask students, "How many counters balanced the toy altogether?" Have them compare this result with their estimate.

Variations

- ❏ Have students place a large heavy object in one side of a bucket balance. Then have them select small heavy objects to add to the other side after each dice throw. (e.g., a brick and bolts)
- ❏ Have students place a light object in one side of a rocker balance. Then have them select light objects to add to the other side after each dice throw. (e.g., a pair of scissors and buttons)

#3532 Math in Action

How Many?

Skills

- ❏ Use informal units to estimate and measure mass
- ❏ Select an appropriate informal unit to measure mass
- ❏ Record mass measurements using tallying

Grouping

- ❏ small groups

Materials

- ❏ balances
- ❏ informal mass units (e.g., large shells, marbles, craft sticks)
- ❏ small, medium, large objects
- ❏ paper and pencils
- ❏ Informal Units Cards copied onto red paper (page 89)
- ❏ Objects Cards copied onto yellow paper (page 90)

Directions

- ❏ Tell students that one way to measure the heaviness of an object is to find out how many smaller objects balance it.
- ❏ Ask students, "How many shells do you think will balance this book?" Discuss and then check.
- ❏ Ask students, "With what else could you try to balance the book? Could you try buttons?" (e.g., "They may be too light, you might need too many.) Could you try rocks?" (e.g., "They may be too heavy.) Justify your suggestions. When you measure the mass of an object, try to use a suitable smaller object as a unit."
- ❏ Review how to use tally marks to keep count of units.
- ❏ Form small groups. Have students explore different ways to measure the mass of an object using informal units. (e.g., Group A may use heavy objects and a bucket balance. Group B may use very light objects and a balance scale. Group C may use medium objects. Group D may explore continuous materials like cups of water or rice to balance an object.)
- ❏ Discuss discoveries and problems together. Have students record their most interesting ones.

Variations

- ❏ Have students shuffle the Informal Units Cards and turn over the top card. Have them shuffle the Objects Cards and turn over the top card. (e.g., rocks and an apple) Ask students, "Are rocks suitable units? Why? Why not? Have them estimate how many units they will need to balance the object.
- ❏ Have students make their own cards, based on objects available in the classroom.

Informal Units Cards

large wooden blocks	marbles

different size rocks	spools
	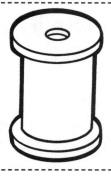
bathroom tiles	shells (different sizes, shapes)

bottle tops	pine cones

paper clips	building blocks
	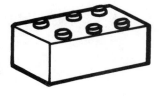

89

Objects Cards

apple	shoe
baseball hat	orange
banana	toy
brick	garbage can
pencil	book

90

Fat Cats

Skills

- ❑ Solve problems using mass concepts
- ❑ Work cooperatively in a team

Grouping

- ❑ pairs
- ❑ small groups

Materials

- ❑ Fat Cats problem (page 92)

Directions

- ❑ Discuss your pets. Ask students, "Would your pet be the heaviest? Why? Whose pet would be the lightest? Why?"

- ❑ Tell students to imagine they are vets. They have to give medicine to each animal according to how heavy it is. A customer comes in with four very fat cats. Ask students, "How could you put them in order according to heaviness?"

- ❑ Discuss suggestions.

- ❑ Look at the Fat Cats problem (page 92). Have students cut out the cat name cards and use them to solve the problem. Discuss the problem in the students' own words. Ask, "How can you find your answer?"

- ❑ Have students work together to find a solution. Ask them, "What different strategies do you use?"

- ❑ Have students check their solution against each statement.

- ❑ When they are convinced their solution is correct, see if they can discover another possibility.

Variation

- ❑ Tell students to invent their own problem about heavy animals for another team to solve. Try to make it have more than one solution.

There are four fat cats.

The cats' names are Tom, Ming, Sam, and Puss.

Tom is heavier than Ming.

Puss is not the lightest.

Sam is lighter than Ming.

Which cat is the heaviest?

Tom	Ming
Sam	Puss

Skills Record Sheet

EXPLORING LENGTH AND AREA

Length									
Constructs, describes, and recognizes long/short lengths									
Constructs, describes, and recognizes high/low lengths									
Constructs, describes, and recognizes thick/thin lengths									
Constructs, describes, and recognizes wide/narrow lengths									
Constructs, describes, and recognizes deep/shallow depths									
Describes and recognizes near/far distances									
Compares and describes two lengths									
Matches baselines to make comparisons									
Compares and describes two perimeters									
Identifies objects with the same length									
Orders three or more lengths									
Uses informal units to estimate and measure straight lengths									
Uses informal units to estimate and measure curves									
Uses informal units to estimate and measure perimeters									
Orders three or more lengths using informal units									
Measures and estimates using meters									
Estimates and measures to the nearest half and quarter meter									
Orders three or more lengths using meters									
Area									
Describes and sorts surfaces using area language									
Recognizes and constructs open/closed lines									
Compares the size of two areas									
Orders three or more areas									
Uses informal units to estimate and measure areas									
Orders three or more areas using informal units									

93

Skills Record Sheet

EXPLORING VOLUME AND MASS

NAME

Volume									
Observes and discusses the space occupied by objects									
Fills and empties containers using a variety of materials									
Packs a variety of objects iinto defined spaces									
Uses volume and capacity language (e.g., *pack, fill, empty*)									
Compares and describes two or more volumes and capacities									
Identifies objects with the same volume and capacity									
Understands that objects with same volume and capacity may have different shapes									
Uses informal units to estimate and measure volume and capacity									
Records volume and capacity measurements using tallying									
Compares volumes by water displacement (rising levels)									
Compares volumes by water displacement (overflow)									
Compares volumes by water displacement (falling levels)									
Understands that volumes stay the same when broken into smaller parts									
Mass									
Uses mass language (e.g., *heavy, light*)									
Lifts to compare two or more masses									
Understands that size is not always related to mass									
Uses an equal-arm balance to compare masses									
Predicts and interprets actions of an equal-arm balance									
Orders three or more masses by lifting; checks using a balance									
Uses informal units to estimate and measure mass									
Selects an appropriate informal unit to measure mass									
Records mass measurements using tallying									
Solves problems using mass concepts									
Works cooperatively in a team									

#3532 Math in Action

Sample Weekly Lesson Plan

STRAND Measurement
GRADE 1

SUBSTRAND Length—Comparing Lengths
TERM 1 **WEEK** 3

SKILLS

- Compare and describe two lengths
- Match baselines to make comparisons
- Compare and describe two perimeters
- Identify objects with same length
- Order three or more lengths

RESOURCES

craft sticks, rods
multilinks, building blocks

string

LANGUAGE

- "about the same length as"
- "exactly the same length as"
- "shorter than", "longer than"
- "taller/shorter than", "almost as tall/short as"

small lengths
(paper clips, pens)
medium lengths
(ribbon, rulers, straws)
large lengths
(string, ropes, shoelaces)

paper squares
masking tape
string
scissors

straws
ping-pong balls
snails
toy cars

MONDAY	TUESDAY	WEDNESDAY	THURSDAY	FRIDAY
• Whole class: Surprise me with what you know about length (open discussion). • Compare student heights. • Rotating Groups: Build tallest tower (five minute time limit) using craft sticks, rods, multi-link, or building bricks. • Whole class: Strategies used by tallest tower team.	• Whole class: How do you know something is exactly the same length as another object? Find pairs of objects exactly the same length. • Pair Activity: Walking Around (page 17)—measure and compare perimeter parts with string. • Whole class: Estimate lengths exactly equal to the length around a playground tree.	• Whole class: Focus on shorter than/longer than, not as long as, just a bit shorter than, etc. • Rotating Groups: Order lengths of three random objects (small, medium, large lengths). • Make It Longer (page 15) • Create a class display of page 16 work.	• Whole class: Focus on ordering irregular lengths. • How do we measure these? How do we know which one is longer? (masking tape shapes on floor) • Jungle Paths worksheet (page 18)	• Whole class: Summarize length issues raised througout the week. • Group Length Challenges (page 19) - How far can you blow? - How far can it swim? - How far can it crawl? - How far can it roll? • Discuss issues arising from group activities.

Weekly Lesson Plan

STRAND _____ SUBSTRAND _____

GRADE _____ TERM _____ WEEK _____

LANGUAGE _____

SKILLS

RESOURCES

MONDAY	TUESDAY	WEDNESDAY	THURSDAY	FRIDAY